A Journey into the World of Cryptocurrency

Anthony Massad

The vast web; a Type 1 civilization technology

"Cryptocurrency is money for the people, by the people."

-The Author

Disclaimer

This book is presented solely for educational and entertainment purposes. The author and publisher are not offering it as legal, accounting, or other professional services advice. While best efforts have been used in preparing this book, the author and publisher make no representations or warranties of any kind and assume no liabilities of any kind with respect to the accuracy or completeness of the contents and specifically disclaim any implied warranties of merchantability or fitness of use for a particular purpose. Neither the author nor the publisher shall be held liable or responsible to any person or entity with respect to any loss or incidental or consequential damages caused, or alleged to have been caused, directly or indirectly, by the information or programs contained herein. No copyright infringement is intended.

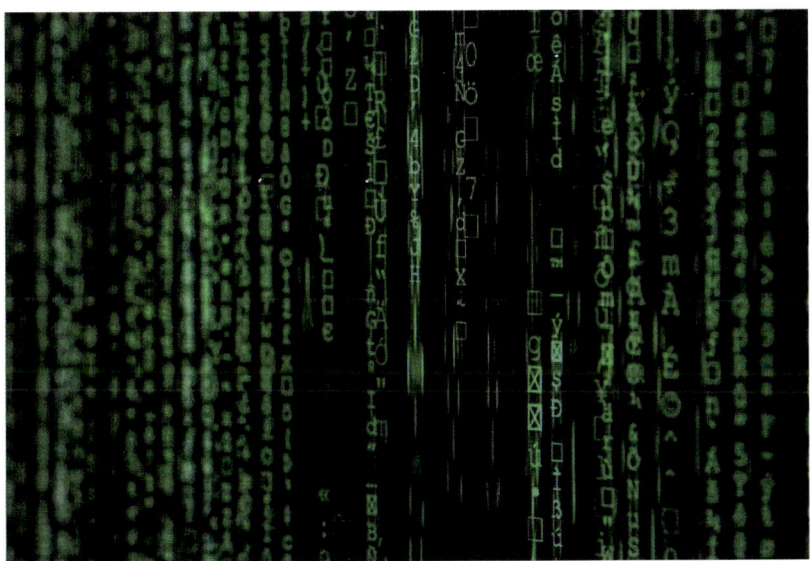

Crypto-Contents

Preface	**vi**
1. Cryptography	**1**
A. The origin to modern day	2
B. Cryptocurrency	3
C. The blockchain	5
2. Who makes the rules?	**8**
A. What is money?	9
B. What backs what?	10
C. Pros & cons of cryptocurrencies	12
3. Crypto-investing	**16**
A. What? Why? Who? How?	17
B. Tony's checklist	18
C. Crypto-exchanges	23
D. Initial coin offering (ICO)	25
E. Day & night trading	26
F. Volatility	28
G. Laws and regulation	30
H. Scams	31
I. Bookkeeping	32
4. Mining	**34**
A. What is mining?	35
B. How to mine?	36

C. Catch 22	37
D. Mobile mining	38

5. Storage & security 40
A. Cryptocurrency wallets	41
B. 2FA (Two Factor Authentication)	43
C. Offline storage	44

6. The future of cryptocurrency: Tony's theory 45
A. Will it last?	46

Crypto-glossary 49

References 55

Preface

Thank you for picking up my book and giving my words and ideas a chance. This book is merely a culmination of my experience in the world of cryptocurrencies and investing that I would like to share with you. This book is not intended to tell you what to invest in but rather developing a mindset and principles about cryptocurrency investing that I found useful based on my experience.

As a member of the millennial generation and being an engineer with a broad technical background, I firmly believe cryptocurrencies will be a major part of our day-to-day lives very soon. I have always been a supporter of rapidly adopting new potentially effective technologies, with cryptocurrency being one of them. Cryptocurrencies will allow wealth to be spread liquidly around the world just as easily as the internet does with information and communication. It will accelerate people's lives and the overall global economy. Cryptocurrency will eventually become as commonly used as the internet.

Advancements in technology are the tools that allow humans to increase productivity, work capacity, efficiency, and effective output. Our world is constantly growing and naturally becoming more demanding for improvements and inventions. This requires constant innovation in creating and improving technologies and processes. I believe our currency system needs innovation.

Also, to note, if you don't understand a specific word, there is a glossary at the end of the book, if your answer isn't there, research it online.

This book is not the end all be all. I encourage you to take your due diligence to research on your own and continue learning long after you read this book. The principles in this book are not only applicable to cryptocurrencies but investing in general. I truly hope you learn and enjoy reading it!

CHAPTER 1
CRYPTOGRAPHY

1.A The origin to modern day

It all began with ancient civilizations use of classic cryptography to hide and communicate secret messages between one another. The ancient Egyptians used hieroglyphics to encrypt and communicate messages throughout time. Julius Caesar, the dictator of Rome, utilized a classical cipher to communicate secret messages to his military generals.

Today, we have wonderful tools, such as computers, which allow us to perform lengthy computations, cre-ate digital products, write code and software with great complexity and efficiency. This has resulted in the rapid acceleration of many sciences. One of those sciences being modern cryptography; constructing and analyzing protocols that prevent third parties from reading or understanding private information.

Various aspects of information security such as data integrity, data confidentiality, non-repudiation, and au-thentication are central to modern cryptography. Modern cryptography is heavily based on mathematical theory and computer science. Cryptographic algorithms are designed around computational hardness assumptions, making them extremely difficult for third parties to crack (decode). Computers can be used to write and encrypt information at a highly advanced faster rate comparable to what any human could do by manual methods. This allows cryptography to have far greater capabilities than ever before. From cryptography, stems the branches of cryptocurrency.

1.B CRYPTOCURRENCY

Cryptocurrency is essentially a peer-to-peer digital currency that keeps each user anonymous from end to end. When a cryptocurrency transaction takes place, the information is stored on a public ledger that cannot be edited, tweaked, or reversed. A public ledger is a decentralized record-keeping system used to store the transactions. Decentralized, meaning there is no middle party facilitating the transaction, essentially no third party takes a cut or fee.

For a digital currency to qualify as a cryptocurrency, it must have its own unique encrypted language, be decentralized, and have a public ledger where all the transactions are stored and cannot be altered. Using Bitcoin as a fundamental example, when a transaction occurs, it is mined (computed) on computers or graphics processing units (GPUs) dispersed somewhere in the world. The information is then stored in a series of digital blocks that cannot be changed. This cuts transaction costs and eliminates the need for a middle party such as a banking institution or a credit card company. This gives the user complete control and the full value of their cryptocurrency. The user is essentially their own bank.

1.C THE BLOCKCHAIN

You may have heard of the term 'blockchain' while reading elsewhere about cryptocurrencies. A blockchain is a digitized public ledger of cryptocurrency transactions. It is simply a series of digital blocks that are created one after another, connected and secured by a cryptographic language. Each block formed in sequence contains a similar a string of code, known as a hash, to the block generated before it. A hash is essentially a timestamp, a link to the previous block, and any other important miscellaneous transaction data. Here is an example of a hash, specifically a SHA-256 (32-byte) hash value:
c5a8d95238cd3ee8c28a86b7ef8553a7c27ac016577c7717b52c-69fa4f721b7f

Can you guess what message this hash has encrypted?

It encrypts my nickname, "Tony".

These codes are inherently resistant to modification after being created because of their unique encryption and formation of blocks which makes them difficult to crack or manipulate.

Blockchains are highly beneficial because they eliminate the double spending problem. The same two blockchains cannot co-exist simultaneously. For example, when I send an email, I am sending a copy of that email, not the original email itself. Now the email is existing in more than one place at one time. If emails followed the same principals as cryptocurrency, then once I send the email, I am no longer in possession of it. With cryptocurrency the double spending problem does not happen because of the blockchain protocol. When one sends cryptocurrency to a specific location, the actual cryptocurrency is sent. The cryptocurrency can exist only in one place at one time. Eliminating the double spending problem is desirable because it can create inflation.

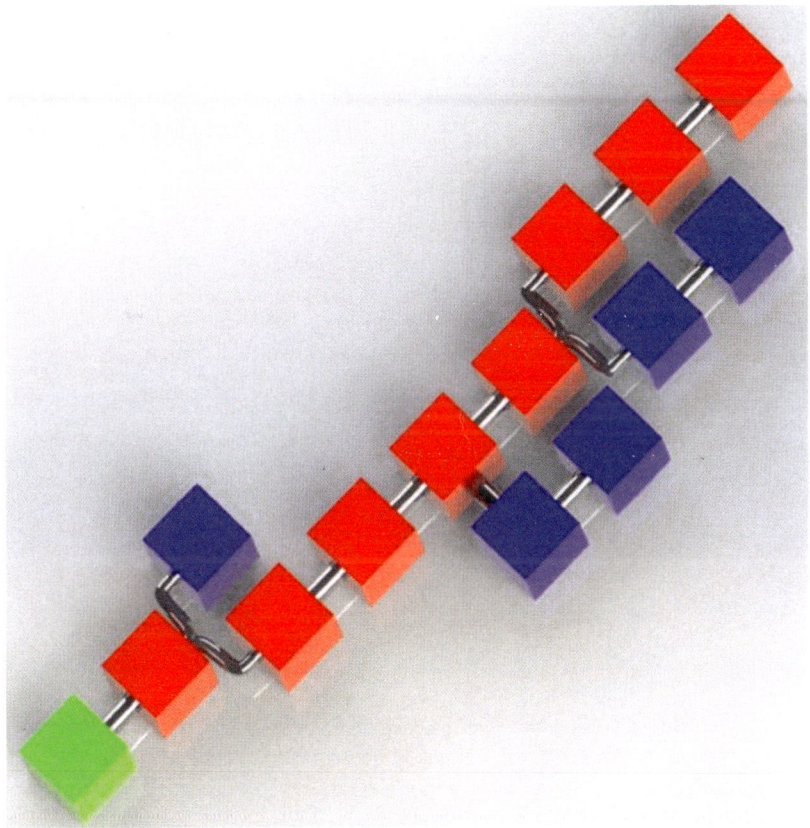

Blockchain formation: The chain begins with the genesis block (green) then connects to the main chain (red), which consists of the longest series. Orphan blocks (blue) are validated and verified but are rejected by the main chain. Each block contains a similar hash to the block generated before it.

"Cryptocurrency has the full potential to change how we exchange goods and services by decentralizing corrupt systems."

-Nirav Patel, Computer Scientist

Chapter 2
Who makes the rules?

2.A What is money?

First, let's define money. We live in a token-based global economy. Essentially, we use currency as a medium to exchange goods and services throughout the globe. In the ancient times people would barter goods and services in exchange for other goods and services. As societies grew, the need for goods and services naturally also grew, and the traditional barter system was no longer feasible. Humans started from the barter system to now paying via electronic methods. Advancements in our civilization's currency systems has allowed us to exchange goods and services far more efficiently.

2.B What backs what?

Personally, I have always wondered what backs the U.S dollar and what controls its value? I've always thought it was gold and other precious metals. The U.S. dollar was backed up by gold until President Nixon took it off the gold standard in 1971.

The term "fiat" translates to "be done or made" in Latin. Fiat currency gives the federal reserve control over the economy because they control how much money is printed. The only reason fiat currency has any value whatsoever is because the federal reserve maintains that value. It is similar to the game of Monopoly, except it is real life and those dollars are honored as real forms of payment.

Personally, I think money should be backed up by a precious finite commodity and by the natural movement of the economy around that commodity. It is important to also note that printing excessive money can create a scary thing called hyperinflation. In economics, hyperinflation is rapid accelerating inflation, which quickly diminishes the real value of currency as the prices of all goods and services rise. Hyperinflation is a quick and easy way to destroy an economy. With cryptocurrency there is a finite amount of it that can exist, and its value is determined by its users' support and a finite circulating supply. For example, there is a finite number of Bitcoins that can exist, 21,000,000 to be exact. Even having millions of dollars saved in the bank can be rendered worthless because the dollar is controlled by a central party that can regulate its value by simply printing more.

    Many people often invest their money into assets that maintain their value regardless of inflation. During economic downturns, investors often look for assets that maintain their value. For example, gold and other precious metals, properties, land, stable coins usually maintain their value during times of inflation. When you save money, do you want your money to have less or more buying power in the future? Personally, I want my money to be able to buy more later.

2.C Pros & cons of cryptocurrencies

The pros:
- Lower transaction costs
- Fraud proof
- Instantaneous, or near instant transactions
- Decentralization: no need for a middle party
- End-to-end assurance
- No permission needed (permissionless)
- Secure encryption
- Pseudonymous (both parties of transaction remain anonymous)
- Full control

Being decentralized, a user does not need authorization from any entity to exchange cryptocurrencies, allowing money to be sent anywhere in the world, requiring an internet connection and a computer or smartphone.

In 2010 when the catastrophic earthquake happened in Haiti, the credit card companies Visa, MasterCard, Discover, and American Express waived their processing fees for select Haiti relief charities. This resulted in the charities receiving the full value of each dollar donated. This is unlikely to happen for all charity relief in the future to come. When using credit card services, about 98% of the payment makes it to the designated destination while the other 2% is used to cover transaction costs and fees. What if there is a way to lessen the transaction fees? With cryptocurrency there is.

Cryptocurrencies also have transaction fees, known as a block fee or mining fee, a burn rate, a gas price (Ethereum). Basically, each cryptocurrency has its own science of how it is transacted. Cryptocurrency transaction fees are determined by a multitude of different factors which is a topic that needs its own book, to say the least. Crypto fees rise and fall. The average cryptocurrency transaction fee generally increases with mass adoption, as it has with Bitcoin. Cryptocurrency fees are still significantly lower than credit card fees.

If a business utilizes a cryptocurrency as a form of sending and receiving payments, it allows the business to save significant amounts of money on transaction fees. If an entity is making millions of global transactions a day, saving just 1% on each transaction can save a significant sum of money. I trade Litecoin, Ethereum, Bitcoin Cash, and XRP due to their transaction fees being far less than the typical 2% credit card fee. I do not purchase Bitcoin, nor do I own it, or plan on owning it. I like Bitcoin as the initial idea and concept it started as, but I believe there are better and more useful alternative cryptocurrencies.

There are benefits and drawbacks to everything in life, cryptocurrency is no different.

The cons:

- No central body regulation
- Unrecognized by several businesses as a legal form of payment
- Volatility: large fluctuations in value
- Uncertainty about the future of cryptocurrencies
- Unclear laws and taxes
- Government scrutiny
- Scrutiny in general
- Hackers
- Can be destroyed by an EMP (electromagnetic pulse)

Cryptocurrency gets a bad reputation for several reasons. Secure and private transactions can make it much easier for people to jump around the law. There is a lot of negative connotation regarding cryptocurrency mainly because it is used throughout the dark web and on various black markets, making it difficult to trace and regulate.

Like all technologies, cryptocurrency can be used for both good and evil. It truly depends on the user's intentions. Using nuclear fission as an example, the technology was used as a weapon of mass destruction (nuclear bomb) to kill millions of human beings. However, this was not the original intent of why it was created. That same technology is used in nuclear medicine, which allows doctors to quickly and accurately diagnose and treat cancer patients. I know I went off on a tangent for a moment there, but the point I was trying to get across is it truly depends on how the technology is used. The same goes for cryptocurrency.

CHAPTER 3

Crypto-investing

3.A What? Why? Who? How?

What, why, who, and how? These are questions I always ask myself when looking into a new investment in order to get a better sense of direction. For starters, I only put in what I am willing to lose completely, and money that I do not need to sustain my lifestyle and pay my bills for a minimum of six months. Personally, any capital I put into cryptocurrency I am holding for the long run. Keep in mind when you are investing the market, you are investing in the future of that market. It also depends on your time horizon and goal. I began with focused investments and then transitioned to a diversified strategy. I came up with a simple checklist to help clarify how to approach investing.

3.B Tony's checklist

There are hundreds of cryptocurrency markets, and thousands of cryptocurrencies, it can be daunting and overwhelming. My method is using a simple checklist. Since you are reading my book, I will share it with you. My simple checklist helps me make investing decisions in general. Keep in mind, this is not the end all be all, you should come up with your own questions in addition as well. Also, be careful of falling in the trap of paralysis by analysis, being overly cautious has its downfalls.

- ✓ What is my investing time horizon?
- ✓ How much risk am I willing to take?
- ✓ How much can I afford to lose?
- ✓ When will I want to pull my earnings out?
- ✓ What do I plan to use my earnings for?
- ✓ Does the cryptocurrency serve a useful purpose and solve a real-world problem?
- ✓ What value does it bring to its users and the world?
- ✓ How can it bring value into my life?
- ✓ Who is the team behind the cryptocurrency and what is their vision?
- ✓ Do I believe in the vision? Is it a realistic and plausible?
- ✓ Does the team who created it have real identities?
- ✓ How and why are they qualified to be developing it?
- ✓ Why would I invest in it or use it?
- ✓ Do I see myself as a user of this product?
- ✓ Does the cryptocurrency cater to a potentially large market? (is it too niche?)
- ✓ Would it make sense for people and industries to adapt, trust, and use this product?

- ✓ Does it currently have large community support?
- ✓ How has it maintained support and presence?
- ✓ Has it withstood the test of time?
- ✓ Is the cryptocurrency legitimate?
- ✓ What is my gut feeling?
- ✓ What do my heart and mind tell me?
- ✓ Is it too good to be true?
- ✓ Does it have a website?
- ✓ Is there a detailed white paper (infopaper) on the cryptocurrency?
- ✓ How does the blockchain protocol work?
- ✓ Can anyone learn to use it?
- ✓ How is it mined or computed?
- ✓ Is it centralized or decentralized?
- ✓ What do the numbers look like?
- ✓ How has it performed in the past?
- ✓ Does it a have a strong track record?

Many fake cryptocurrencies have a website but do not have a team, or any human identity attached to the website, this is very common. I stay away. Keep in mind that just because it is listed on a crypto-exchange or website does not mean its legitimate.

I always take time to read the whitepaper. A cryptocurrency white paper is a document that explains the protocol of the cryptocurrency. Like a startup company trying to raise capital, it provides a definition of the problem it is trying to solve and how it will go about solving the problem. Also, it usually should contain technical information on how the cryptocurrency works. I always check, read and examine the whitepaper thoroughly for all cryptocurrencies I am looking to possibly invest in. If a cryptocurrency does not have a whitepaper or does have one but it provides little to no information, this is a red flag.

A good indicator is the cryptocurrency gaining steady value over time: nothing worthwhile happens overnight, easy come, easy go. I always examine the numbers; they tell the truth.

Here is a funny but horrible story of how I got burned (not actually physically burned) from a scam cryptocurrency. I was a blind and dumb investor at the time. Paccoin, once had large community and market support, including myself. The Paccoin developers issued a hard fork (a coin swap) for the old Paccoins for new updated Paccoins to a 1000:1 ratio. After the hard fork of Paccoin, it resulted in everyone losing virtually all of their value in Paccoin. Paccoin turned out to be a scam. I had several thousands in USD of Paccoin and lost 1000% value after the hard fork. This lesson costed me, but it was not in vain because I learned a valuable lesson and grew wiser from it. Each disappointment I face is a fruit of wisdom. I learn best and the most when I fail. Even though Paccoin had large support it turned out to be a scam coin in the end that robbed everyone. It doesn't take long to realize that the world is catered to sheep, just because the herd follows doesn't mean it is the right way. Avoid being fooled by logical fallacies; the bandwagon fallacy. You would think most people would have financial common sense, but they don't. Financial common sense is very uncommon.

I think of each cryptocurrency as a start-up company. Start-up companies are known for high ambition and high failure rates; therefore, I invest accordingly and wisely. I will never invest into a cryptocurrency because someone else said "it's a good idea". I make my own logical, rational, calculated financial decisions. I do not take on risk blindly. Blind investing is an easy path to destruction. Avoid investing based off opinions, stick to using facts and numbers. Understanding the difference between facts and opinions is critical. I cannot stress it enough. Most people who fail in the investment world fail because they invest based off words and opinions. I always examine and see what the numbers are saying. The numbers tell you what is happening.

There is a ton of over-hype in the crypto market, as there is in any market. Marketing is really the science of hype and appealing to people's emotions. I do my best to manage my trades with little emotion, sticking to the facts, data, and numbers. I process all information as information and avoid letting emotions cloud my judgement and ultimately influence my actions. I do not invest based on other people's opinions, only my opinion. I keep an open mind, listen, and act on my own. Sleeping on my decisions has helped me immensely, time and time again. I never invest into anything the first day I learn about it, to me this is madness. I look at investing like a roller coaster and knowing when to jump on at the lowest or highest point, or just riding it out and seeing where it takes me. For me, time in the market is more important than timing the market.

Take your time and due diligence to research and educate yourself before jumping into any investment and spending your money. If you think something deserves your investment, you deserve to be educated and informed about every detail.

3.C CRYPTO-EXCHANGES

A digital cryptocurrency exchange (crypto-exchange) is an online market platform where a user can buy, sell, and trade cryptocurrencies. There are several different crypto-exchanges that currently exist and new ones constantly in the making. I used Bitstamp as my first step to embark into the crypto-investing world because it seemed legitimate and was the easiest method to setup and trade my USD for cryptocurrency. Crypto-exchanges will ask you for personal information to verify your identity. Many people do not like the verification process due to having to release personal information (ID, driver's license front & back, D.O.B).

There are hundreds of different crypto-exchanges, and they all offer and trade different cryptocurrencies. For example, Coinbase currently only trades around 17 cryptocurrencies such as Bitcoin, Ethereum, Litecoin, Bitcoin Cash, Ripple (XRP), and several more. I personally never initially trade my fiat currency for Bitcoin as I lose a lot of money due to the mining costs. When I initially convert my fiat money, I usually buy Litecoin, Ripple (XRP), or Ethereum. Those seem to be universally accepted on most other crypto-exchanges.

After Bitstamp, I started trading on Cryptopia and Binance. These cryp-to-exchanges sell several different altcoins (alternative cryptocurrencies) that Bitstamp did not offer. I send my cryptocurrency to a virtual wallet on those market platforms to be able to trade it with other altcoins. The other exchanges must have a specific cryptocurrency wallet for the cryptocurrency

Keep in mind, just because an altcoin is listed on a crypto-exchange does not mean it is legitimate. Not all crypto-exchanges to take the due diligence to do a back-ground check to determine whether a cryptocurrency is fraudulent or not. Be aware of this.

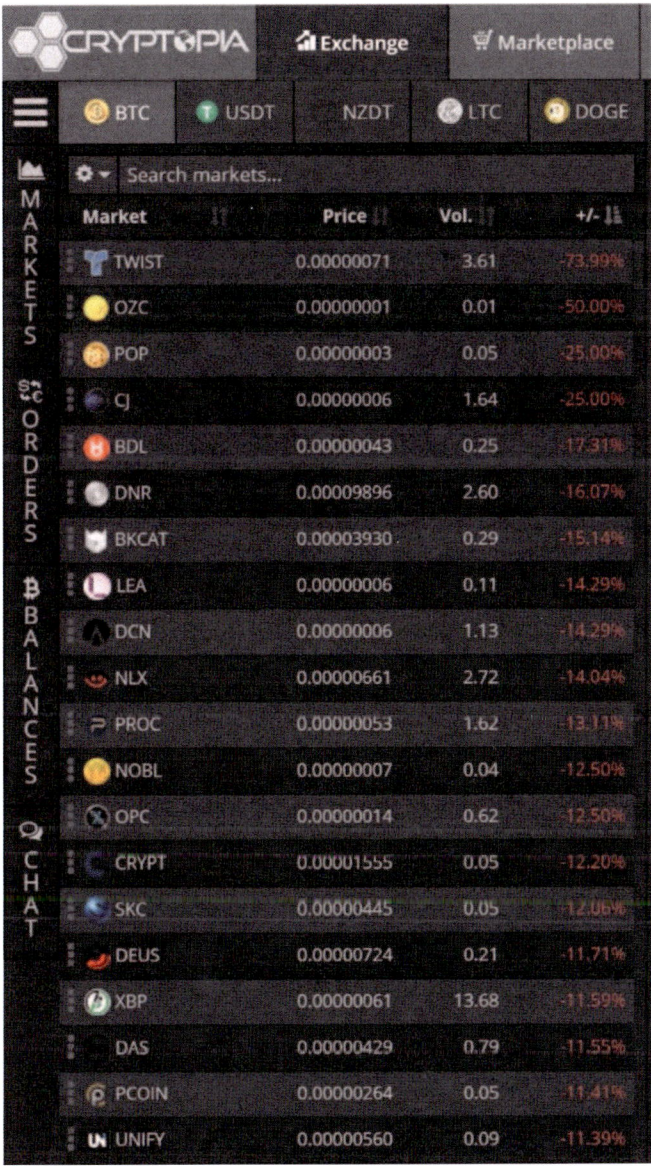

3.D INITIAL COIN OFFERING (ICO)

Often times I will see and hear the term ICO (initial coin offering), this is similar to an IPO (initial public offering) in stocks. This is when a company tries to raise initial capital by selling its shares or stocks at a cheaper price. When a new cryptocurrency hits the market most of them start out with an ICO. The problem with ICO's is that several companies have scammed investors into sending them free money with fake schemes. ICO's have thus been outlawed in the United States and several other countries.

A famous scam that occurred in November of 2017 was Confido. Confido was running an ICO and raised about $375,000 from investors. Shortly after the ICO the Confido team disappeared. The coin was being traded around $1.20 and then took a dive to about 2 cents a coin. The firm's website and all traces of social media accounts were deleted and erased. Beware of ICO's, there is no way for investors to protect themselves from ICO fraud. Once a user's cryptocurrency is sent to an ICO address or any address there is nothing the user can do to get it back.

3.E Day & night trading

No one can ever predict what the market will do exactly. I use fundamental trading principals as if I was trading on the traditional stock market. This book does not intend to teach you how to day and night trade cryptocurrencies. Keep in mind the traditional stock market is open typically 9:30 a.m. to 4:00 p.m. The crypto currency markets operate 24 hours a day all year around. Day and night trading cryptocurrency can be a daunting task, it is like fighting the lion for scraps. My objective is to typically invest in a worthy cryptocurrency and hold onto it for my established time horizon. I do not to lose sleep over cryptocurrency or let it control my life. If my investment causes me to lose sleep, then it is likely not a good investment to begin with.

Many people often tell me crypto-investing is risky, stocks are risky, or building a business is risky. I personally think the highest risk anyone can take is living on one stream of income for their entire lives. Our modern-day conventional thinking is to go to school, get a degree, get a career, start a 401K, invest in the stock market, and then retire at 65. Do what the majority does, and you get the majority's results. Don't get me wrong, I went to school, I got an engineering degree, participated in student organizations, worked at various internships, and got a full – time career. I did all the things society and my parents expected of me. I am not saying to not go to school. School is good, education is valuable, but education should continue long after school is over. Learning about growing other streams of income on the side is a must. The illusion of career safety is nothing more than an illusion.

If you do not have financial literacy and wisdom, all of the money in the world won't do you any good. You must learn how to manage it. Personally, I will learn, build, experience, grind, work my a$$ off, and lose sleep to build my empire. It is your job to make yourself wealthy, not anyone else. I encourage all humans to constantly learn, think, grow, improve their skills, learn new skills, grow in knowledge, wisdom, educate themselves, build a side business, and make wise financial and life decisions. The journey starts with the mindset. In order to change the world around you, you must change the world within you.

3.F VOLATILITY

Cryptocurrencies are extremely volatile and unpredictable. During times of uncertainty there will be volatility. Keep in mind cryptocurrency is still in the early adoption phase at the time I write this. I use the method of dollar cost averaging. I calculate a portion of my disposable income and invest it regardless of what the current market prices are. I know over the long run I will get a much larger return.

There are several computer programs and algorithms that claim to be able to predict how the market will fluctuate in price, but these are not reliable, because predicting the future is unpredictable. The market is mainly controlled by people's emotions. As Isaac Newton once said, *"I can calculate the motion of the heavenly bodies, but not the madness of people",* Sir Isaac Newton.

It is common sense to buy low and sell high, but the majority of people do the exact opposite, due to a number of reasons, but ultimately emotion. Again, when it comes to money, common sense is very uncommon.

Again, the objective is to jump on the roller coaster at the lowest point and jump off at the highest point. The key point is knowing when to jump on and off, aka knowing when to buy low and sell high. I take my profit return and never look back and ponder on how much I could have made if I had held on just a bit longer. Many people have been destroyed by waiting too long, being overly cautious and missing the opportunity. At some point you must jump.

3.G Laws and regulation

The laws and regulation of cryptocurrencies are different throughout each country. In the United States, it is not legal tender according to the Financial Crimes Enforcement Network. In 2014, the IRS (Internal Revenue Service) stated cryptocurrency is not an actual currency but defined it as a property and issued guidance on how it should be taxed. That information can be found on the IRS government website. Government regulators differ in their definitions of Bitcoin and other cryptocurrencies. For example, Japan contains the largest market for Bitcoin, they account for about half of the global trading volume of Bitcoin. Japan marked it as legal tender in 2018. Crypto-exchanges are legal in Japan if they are registered with the Japanese Financial Services agency. Binance, Japan's largest crypto trading market got a lot of heat for not being legally registered for a time.

If you plan to crypto-invest and trade, I recommend doing it legally in compliance of your country's government rules and regulations. Take the time and the due diligence to educate yourself on the rules and regulations put in place by your government.

3.H SCAMS

The trading bot is essentially supposed to be a computer algorithmic code, or an AI (artificial intelligence) that invests the user's money based on calculations it makes in the market. One example of this is the mother of all scams, "Bitconnect", as one can see the logo. Bitconnect in short terms was a highly developed crypto Ponzi scheme. The company claimed to have a trading robot platform that promised impossible payouts (1% daily compounded interest).

The Bitconnect interest greatly fluctuated due to the volatility of Bitcoin which made the 1% daily compounded interest impossible to meet. Bitconnect customers received payouts in Bitconnect's "BCC" proprietary currency, which was all liquidated soon after Bitcoin crashed causing anyone with Bitconnect coin to lose the majority of their value. The former CEO of Bitconnect Carlos Matos can be found on YouTube screaming "BITCOOOON-NECTT!!!!". He is a despicable human being. More details can be found on the internet if you really want to know more about him.

I keep my money out of trading bots. There are no trading bots that are guaranteed you to make money, it is usually a money grab attempt by those companies advertising it. There are several trading bot software applications that one can install on their personal computer. I avoid these because they could contain harmful malware that can steal personal information, vital data, and your money.

3.1 BOOKKEEPING

The cryptocurrency markets run 24 hours a day, seven days a week, 365 days a year globally. A simple way I keep track of my investment portfolio is utilizing cryptocurrency tracking apps. As shown in the picture. Blockfolio is a great app I personally use to keep track of all my cryptocurrency transactions. As soon as I complete a trade, I immediately log the transaction on my Blockfolio app. The trading company "Robinhood" has recently become part of the crypto-game. This app (or company) actually allows you to buy a select number of cryptocurrencies. Keep in mind Robinhood does not contain all the altcoins available on the crypto markets to purchase and track.

When making a trade or purchase of cryptocurrency, I have my smartphone handy with a crypto-tracking app and immediately record the trade in the application. For me, this method is extremely simple and is an easy way to track my investments. You do not have to record your transactions with my method, there are several other methods and platforms to do this as well.

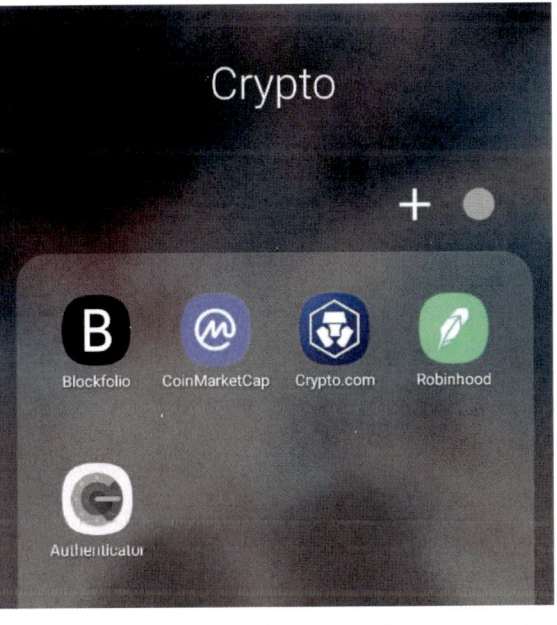

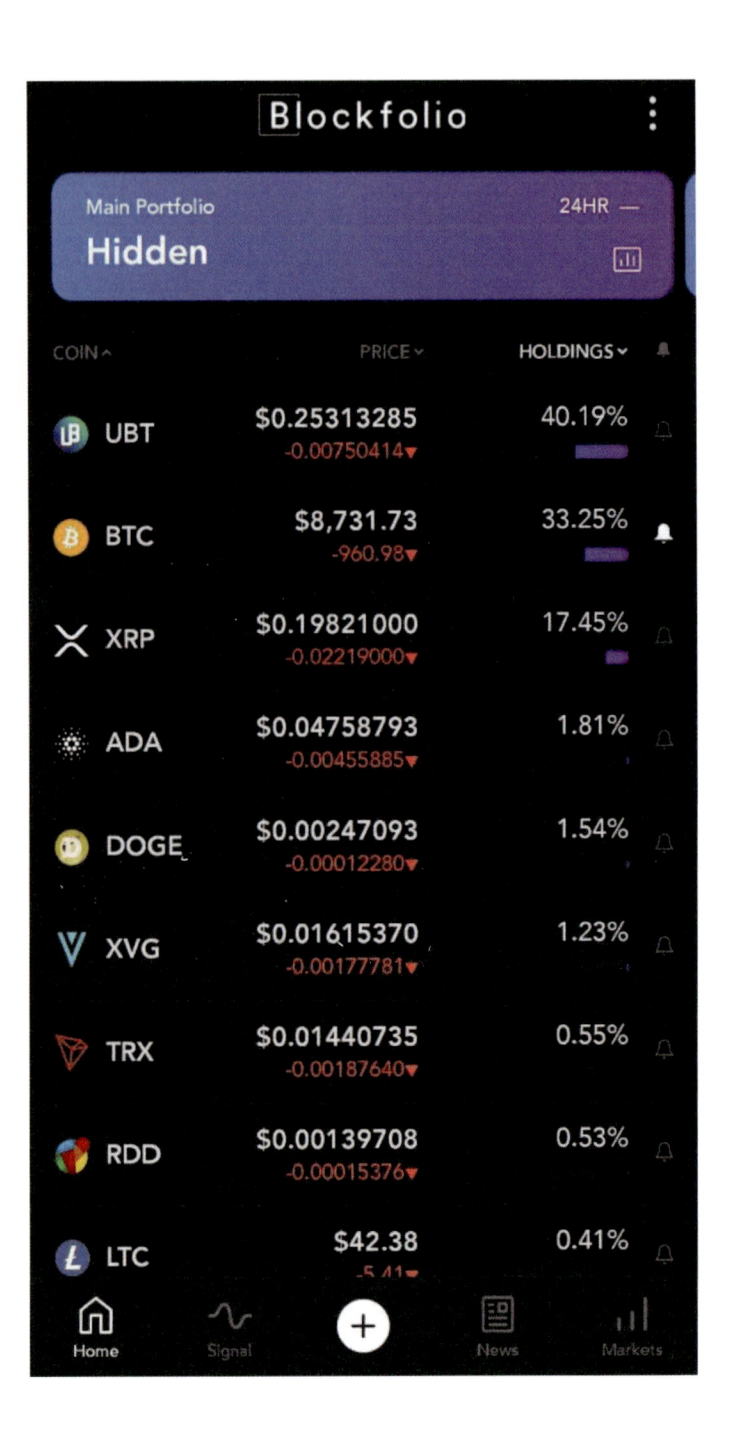

COIN	PRICE	HOLDINGS
UBT	$0.25313285 -0.00750414▼	40.19%
BTC	$8,731.73 -960.98▼	33.25%
XRP	$0.19821000 -0.02219000▼	17.45%
ADA	$0.04758793 -0.00455885▼	1.81%
DOGE	$0.00247093 -0.00012280▼	1.54%
XVG	$0.01615370 -0.00177781▼	1.23%
TRX	$0.01440735 -0.00187640▼	0.55%
RDD	$0.00139708 -0.00015376▼	0.53%
LTC	$42.38 -5.41▼	0.41%

CHAPTER 4
Mining

4.A What is mining?

AT SOME POINT OR another you have probably heard the word "mining" being talked about on the news or by others. Mining in the simplest of terms is the process of a computing cryptocurrency blockchain transactions. As a reward for computing these blocks a very small percentage of that transaction is awarded to the miner, hence the term "mining coins". Myself I have never taken the time to mine cryptocurrency or invest in any mining rigs. I see mining as a different way to invest into cryptocurrencies. I've just never seen a reason for myself to do so in that way. Personally, I'd rather take educated risks on crypto-trading than mining.

4.B How to mine?

Mining requires reasonable background knowledge in computers and the skills to assemble the proper hardware. Basically, a graphics card (GPU), power supply, a motherboard, and a computer to setup the operation. There are several pre-assembled mining machines or rigs available to purchase on the internet. These still require extensive knowledge to setup and run. For those who want to mine but don't know how, there are several resources all over the internet to learn this.

4.C CATCH 22

You might think mining is a great way to make money passively, so what's the catch? The catch is that mining may require powerful and expensive graphics processing units that can consume massive amounts of electricity. I have had friends who have built mining rigs and let them run in their college dorms because they do not have to pay for electricity. There are inconceivably massive Bitcoin mines dispersed around the world mining all day, every day. According to a research paper titled "The Bitcoin Mining Network", China accounts for around 65 percent of Bitcoin mining.

You must do the mathematical analysis on hardware costs, electricity consumption, time, potential earnings, and ultimately determine if it is worth it to mine in your situation.

4.D Mobile mining

Certain cryptocurrencies can be mined on mobile platforms. For example, Electroneum (ETN) is the first of its kind to develop a mobile mining platform on smart phone devices. Computers, tablets, phones can download the Electroneum mining software and begin mining the coin and be rewarded. The payout limit on their mobile platform is around 10 ETN coins. This gives the user an incentive to use their electronic devices to mine ETN while not in use.

There are various other mobile mining apps available on the market but most of them take a long time to mine anything. The catch with mobile mining is that it takes an absurdly long time to mine any value. Mining requires powerful dedicated machines; a mobile phone simply is not powerful enough yet. However, it is not a bad idea for anyone who wants to get their feet wet in the mining world without taking on too much risk or investing a great deal of time and effort.

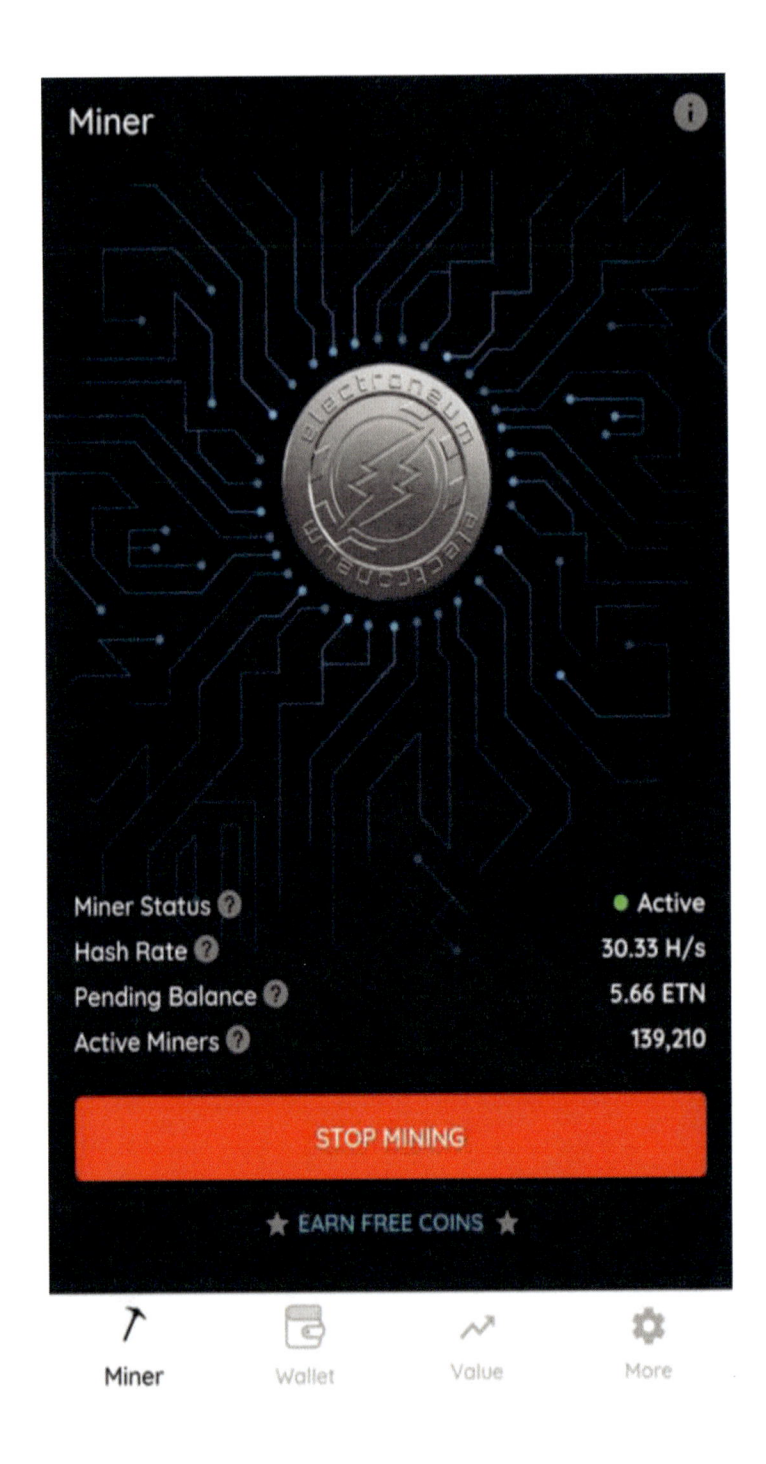

MINING

Miner

Miner Status — ● Active
Hash Rate — 30.33 H/s
Pending Balance — 5.66 ETN
Active Miners — 139,210

STOP MINING

★ EARN FREE COINS ★

Miner   Wallet   Value   More

Chapter 5
Storage & security

5.A Cryptocurrency wallets

Digital cryptocurrency wallets also known as virtual wallets are used to store cryptocurrency on the web at a virtual address. Virtual wallets are usually provided by crypto-exchanges or other 3rd party sites. This is where the user's cryptocurrency is readily available online to trade on the exchange, send or receive to a different address, or do whatever the user desires.

Each wallet has its own specific digital address that is used to send and receive cryptocurrency. Each wallet is biologically specific to the cryptocurrency. For example, I cannot send or store Ethereum in a Bitcoin wallet. I cannot send or store Litecoin into an Ethereum wallet. If I attempt to send cryptocurrency to a wallet address that is not designated for that specific cryptocurrency, it will be lost in limbo. The web wallets provided by the crypto exchange are usually there to store coins for trading or transferring. I however do not consider it a good idea to leave cryptocurrency in the online exchange wallets unless I am going to trade them. Why? There are occurrences where the exchange is hacked, and cryptocurrencies are stolen from the exchange. This can have horrendous consequences. Cryptopia as I mentioned before, is just one of many hacked exchanges. Anyone, who had cryptocurrency on Cryptopia, is still currently locked out at the time I write this.

Important Announcement

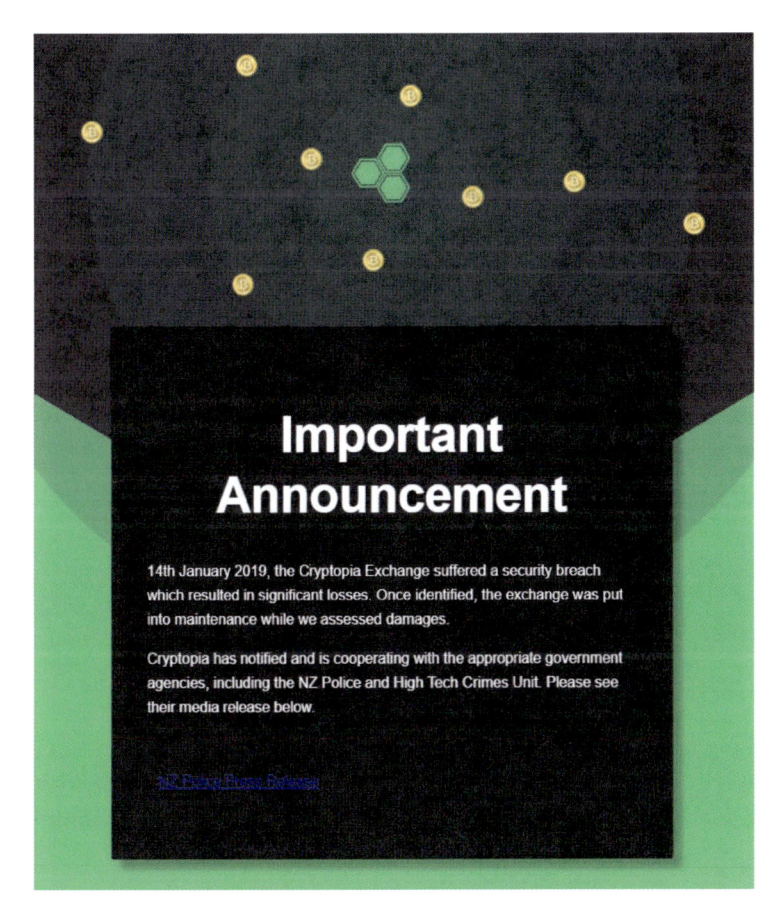

14th January 2019, the Cryptopia Exchange suffered a security breach which resulted in significant losses. Once identified, the exchange was put into maintenance while we assessed damages.

Cryptopia has notified and is cooperating with the appropriate government agencies, including the NZ Police and High Tech Crimes Unit. Please see their media release below.

NZ Police Press Release

The first message Cryptopia sent out when the exchange was hacked. The company was forced to take the exchange offline to prevent anymore losses. It is down until further notice.

5.B 2FA (Two Factor Authentication)

I made a section on 2FA this because I cannot stress it enough to mention the immense and powerful security a two-factor authenticator has. It is an extremely effective and secure method for protecting your assets.

I personally utilize two-factor authentication method to access all of my online accounts for cryptocurrency, stocks, RuneScape, and anything under the sun with an account login. Google Authenticator™ is a 2FA method that is easy to implement.

Many crypto-exchanges have authenticators integrated within their system, and they usually ask to create one by default. Be careful if you decide to factory wipe your phone, as you will lose the authentication code generators in the authentication app and be locked out of your accounts. Save yourself the pain and avoid the hassle of being locked out of your crypto accounts. I had to learn the hard way doing this. It was not an experience I would ever like to repeat.

5.C Offline Storage

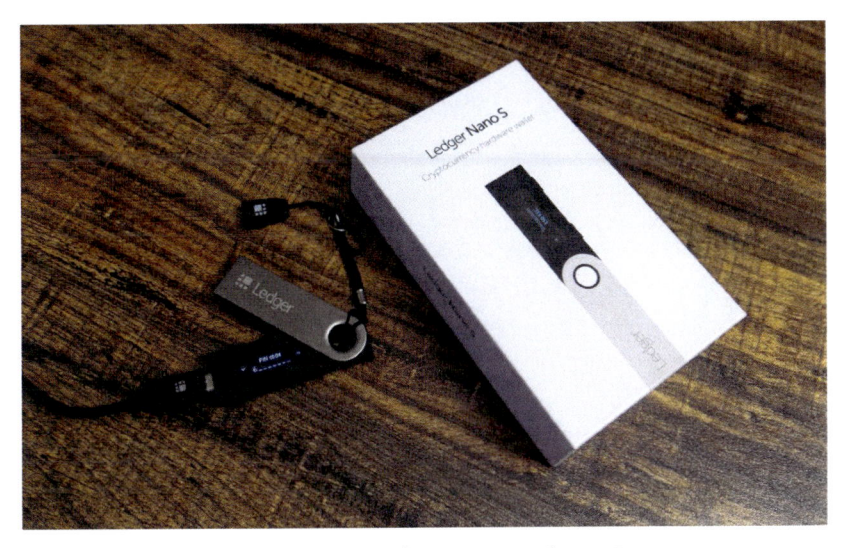

My personal Nano Ledger S cryptocurrency hardware wallet.

In order to protect your investments, it is best to store them on a hardware wallet, also known as a "cold wallet". Above is a picture of the Nano Ledger S, a commonly used and reputable cryptocurrency hardware wallet. There are several different types of hardware wallets, but it is best to go with the one that suits your needs. Not all hardware wallets have the same level of security and support storage of all the cryptocurrencies that exist.

For me, securing my cryptocurrency off the internet is the safest way to avoid having my coins stolen or lost. They are much safer offline. I always make sure to record my passwords and pin codes to avoid risking losing my cryptocurrencies. Personally, I store my hardware wallet in a waterproof plastic bag and tuck it away in a location that only I know of.

Chapter 6

The future of cryptocurrency: Tony's theory

6.A Will it last?

No one can be truly certain about the future of cryptocurrency. I believe the strong will survive and the weak will die. The useful cryptocurrencies will make it big and the ones that provide the least value will bottom out and disappear. I think Bitcoin will end up staying for a while before its supporters realize that there are more efficient cryptocurrencies out there.

At the current moment it is the wild west in the cryptocurrency industry, there will be a lot of carnage before all the sharp edges are smoothed out. There is great support in the crypto-community from not just average people but politicians, powerful business leaders, and entrepreneurs from all over the planet.

There is great room for the cryptocurrency and blockchain industry to grow. I can only speak for myself, but I have found that adopting new technology is a part of everyday life. Millions of people rush to buy the latest smartphone, computer, TV, gaming console, smartphone app, why is cryptocurrency any different?

Throughout history, past civilizations have generally accelerated when they adopt newer technologies. Just recently, humans adopted things like the internet, smartphones, computers, and much more. We can certainly adopt more useful tools to further advance our society every day.

Cryptocurrency vs. Other markets

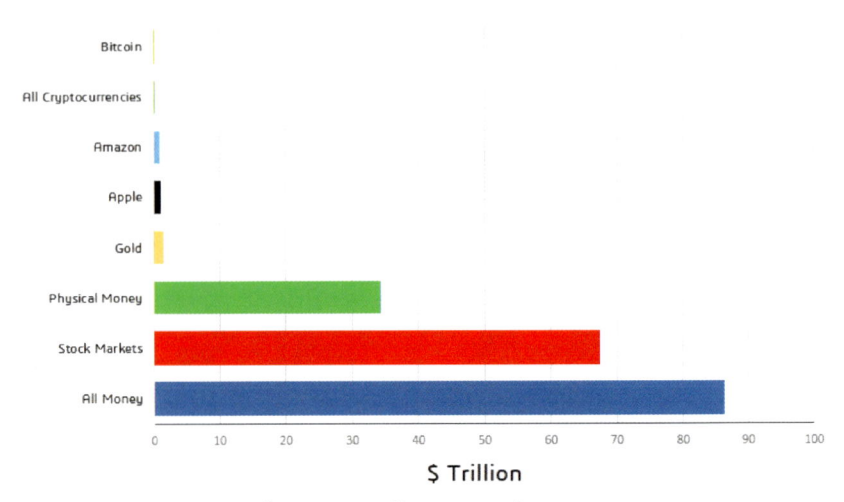

Category	$ Trillion
Bitcoin	~0
All Cryptocurrencies	~0
Amazon	~1
Apple	~1
Gold	~1
Physical Money	~35
Stock Markets	~67
All Money	~87

Values as of September 2018

Here we can see a graphical representation of the cryptocurrency market versus other market assets. Cryptocurrency is tiny speck, still in its infancy with plenty of room to grow. The bubble of cryptocurrencies still has a lot more growing to do before it bursts. Like anything in life, it takes time. The test of time will show what the future will be for cryptocurrencies.

It is a good idea to maintain and work on other streams of income, not just one. Please do not rely on a company, a union, or worse, the government, to protect your financial health and future. Rely on yourself. Myself, I work full time as a mechanical engineer, am a focused stock investor, and have my side business, which all produce streams of income. I am constantly reading, learning, increasing my knowledge and wisdom, and working on ways to maximize my high-income skills. I believe building wealth starts with the mind, and then will perpetuate out into the physical world. The greatest investment I can make, is in myself. In case you have not done so already, build your team by networking with like-minded people who want to become wealthy or who have already attained great wealth in the endeavor you want. What you do in your free time and who you spend your time with determines your future. It is your responsibility to make yourself wealthy.

"Cryptocurrency will revolutionize privacy, fees and transfer speeds which will make the world a better-connected financial entity"

-Jamal Warida, Data Scientist & Mechanical Engineer

CHAPTER 7
CRYPTO-GLOSSARY

(Not all of the crypto terms that exist but mostly the common ones)

- **51% Attack:** a condition in which more than half the computing power on a cryptocurrency network is controlled by a single miner or group of miners. The amount of power gives them control over the network such as, stopping other user's transactions being confirmed, spending the same coins a multiple of times, prevent other miners from mining valid blocks, and issue a transaction that conflicts with someone else's.
- **Address:** a digital address is utilized to send and receive cryptocurrency over the internet. It is also the public key used by the users to digitally sign the transactions.
- **All time high (ATH):** The highest point in price in a cryptocurrency's history.
- **All time low (ATL):** The lowest point in price in a cryptocurrency's history.
- **Altcoin:** a name to describe all the alternative cryptocurrencies to Bitcoin. For example, Reddcoin and Verge are considered altcoins.
- **Bear:** a market in which share prices are on a downward trend.
- **Bitcoin ATM:** a real-life physical machine that allows the user to buy Bitcoin.
- **Block reward:** a reward (small fraction of the trans action) given to the miner after successfully hashing (computing) the transaction block.
- **Blockchain:** a list of blocks that have been mined (computed) since the beginning of the cryptocurrency.
- **Bull:** a market in which share prices are on a positive trend.
- **Burner wallet:** A temporary web wallet used to send

and receive cryptocurrency. It can then be destroyed eliminating transaction history on the public ledger.

- **Centralized:** Controlled by a central group or organization.
- **Cold wallet:** A device that stores cryptocurrency offline.
- **Cryptocurrency:** A digital currency in which cryptography or encryption methods are used to regulate, transfer, and operate without use of a third party or central bank.
- **Cryptography:** A method of encrypting information and communication using a secret code and language.
- **DDoS (Distributed Denial of Service attack):** A cyber-attack in which the attacker's goal is to make the network or machine resources unavailable to its intended users by temporarily or indefinitely disrupting services of who is connected. This is done by the attacker using several systems to flood the bandwidth or resources of the targeted system.
- **Decentralized:** The opposite of centralized, no central party control.
- **Dump:** Selling off most of the user's cryptocurrency in a certain period of time.
- **Exit scam:** A process when a cryptocurrency company vanishes off the face of the internet after they usually have scammed users into buying their cryptocurrency, usually during an initial coin offering.
- **Fiat currency:** Any form of physical paper or metal currency that is regulated and centralized. Examples include USD (American dollar), and EUR (European euro).
- **FOMO syndrome:** Fear of missing out on the next big investment. A form of mass hysteria that happens to many investors.

- **FUD:** Fear, Uncertainty, and Doubt. Feelings felt by many investors.
- **Hard fork:** An occurrence when a single cryptocurrency splits into two. When a change is implemented to the original cryptocurrency blockchain protocol; a permanent divergence in the blockchain protocol. For example, Bitcoin hard forked into Bitcoin Cash, Segwit, Segwit2x, and Bitcoin Gold. Each hard-forked cryptocurrency uses a different code and requires its own specific wallet for that coin. Hard forks are not backwards compatible.
- **Hash:** The act of performing a hash function on input data of arbitrary size with an output of fixed length that looks random, from which no data can be recovered without a cipher.
- **HODL:** A type of investing strategy in which the user holds onto the crypto currency for long term regardless of the price fluctuations in the market. The term originated from a typo in a bitcoin forum, it then became an acronym for "hold on for dear life".
- **ICO (Initial Coin offering):** Just as companies on the traditional stock market use IPOs (initial public offerings), an ICO is essentially the same thing, a crowdfund method using the cryptocurrency to raise capital in the beginning stages of the start-up.
- **Mining difficulty:** A number that describes the level of difficulty to hash (compute) a new block.
- **Node:** A copy of the ledger operated by a participant of the blockchain network.
- **Protocol:** The set of rules that define the interactions on a network, which typically involves a consensus, transaction validation, and network participation on a blockchain.
- **Pump and dump:** A fraudulent scheme involving the artificial inflation of the price of a cryptocurrency. It usually starts with false, misleading positive

statements, like a bunch of fake hype, in order to inflate the cheaply priced cryptocurrency to be sold for a higher price.

- **Shitcoin:** A coin with no obvious value or potential to be valuable. It solves no real-world problem or issue. For example, Dogecoin is an example of a shitcoin.
- **Soft fork:** Similar to a hard fork, this is a change in the cryptocurrencies blockchain protocol wherein only previous valid transactions are made invalid. Soft forks are typically backwards compatible.
- **Stable coin:** A cryptocurrency with very little volatility, it may be backed up by a precious commodity or a fiat currency. Some examples of stable coins include, TrueUSD, and Tether which are backed up by USD.
- **Symbol:** The ticker name used for cryptocurrencies on the crypto-market. For example, Ripple's cryptocurrency is listed as XRP, Litecoin is listed as LTC, and Ethereum is listed as ETH.
- **Token:** A digital unit that hold may or may not hold value on its own but provides access to a larger cryptocurrency economic system.
- **Volatility:** Liability to change rapidly and unpredictably.
- **Volume:** The amount of cryptocurrency that has been traded during a certain period of time. For example, a cryptocurrency with high trading volume within the last 24 hours is more likely to get sold or bought more quickly.
- **Wallet:** A secure digital or hard wallet used to store, send, and receive cryptocurrency.
- **Whale:** An investor who has great amounts of a specific cryptocurrency. Someone who owns so much of that cryptocurrency in which they can manipulate the market prices. A whale because they can literally

make waves in the market.
- **White Paper:** The cryptocurrency infopaper, located on most cryptocurrency websites. It is a document describing the cryptocurrency's protocol in great detail.

References

"Blockfolio." *Blockfolio*, blockfolio.com/.

"Cryptocurrency Market Capitalizations." *CoinMarketCap*, coinmarketcap.com/.

"ELECTRONEUM. THE MOBILE CRYPTOCURRENCY." *Electroneum – The Mobile Based Cryptocurrency,* electroneum.com/.

"Start Trading the World's Largest Range of Cryptocurrencies." Cryptopia - Home, www.cryptopia.co.nz/.

Bitconnect. (n.d.). Retrieved from https://www.worldcoinindex.com/coin/bitconnect

Ledger. "Ledger Nano S." *Ledger,* www.ledger.com/products/ledger-nano-s.

Christopher Bendiksen and Samuel Gibbons. "The Bitcoin Mining Network." 2019. PDF file.

Made in the USA
Las Vegas, NV
08 December 2020